Vietnamesische
Nationalversammlung
in Hanoi
Vietnamese National
Assembly Building
in Hanoi

Meinhard von Gerkan
Nikolaus Goetze

Vietnamesische Nationalversammlung in Hanoi

Vietnamese National Assembly Building in Hanoi

gmp FOCUS

gmp · Architekten von Gerkan, Marg und Partner

Verortung

Location

21° 2' N, 105° 50' O

Im Norden Vietnams, im fruchtbaren Delta des Roten Flusses, liegt Hà Nội, die „Stadt im Fluss". Die Hauptstadt Vietnams blickt auf eine wechselvolle Geschichte zurück: Besatzungen, Kolonialherrschaft, Indochina- und Vietnamkrieg. Diese bewegten Zeiten haben auch das Stadtbild von Hanoi geprägt: Von 1883 bis 1945 war die Stadt das Verwaltungszentrum Französisch-Indochinas. In dieser Zeit entstand südlich des damaligen Stadtkerns ein rechtwinklig angelegtes Netz aus baumgesäumten Boulevards mit Oper, Kirchen und öffentlichen Bauten im Kolonialstil, Teile des historischen Kaiserpalastes und der Zitadelle von Thăng Long mussten weichen. In Alt-Hanoi finden sich jedoch bis heute Spuren aus sehr viel früheren Zeiten: Über tausend Jahre alt ist etwa das Viertel der 36 Gassen, ein verschachteltes Labyrinth mit den traditionellen Rohrhäusern auf schmalem, tiefem Grundriss.

Hà Nội, the "city between the rivers," lies in the north of Vietnam, in the fertile Red River Delta. Vietnam's capital looks back on an eventful history: occupations, colonial rule, the First Indochina War, and the Vietnam War. These turbulent times also shaped the cityscape of Hanoi. From 1883 to 1945, the city was the administrative center of French Indochina. During this period, an orthogonal network of tree-lined boulevards with an opera house, churches, and public buildings in colonial style was built south of what was then the city center; parts of the historic imperial palace and the Citadel of Thăng Long had to make way. In the Old Quarter, however, traces from much earlier times can still be found today: the Thirty-Six Streets district—a convoluted labyrinth with traditional tube houses (nhà ong) on narrow, deep plots—is more than a thousand years old.

Hanoi

Vietnam

Stadt im Fluss

City between the Rivers

Nach der japanischen Besatzung im Zweiten Weltkrieg rief Hồ Chí Minh 1945 die Demokratische Republik Vietnam aus, deren Hauptstadt Hanoi wurde. Es folgten zwei lange Kriege um die Vormachtstellung im geteilten Land. Erst 1975 waren die Kämpfe beendet, es kam zur Wiedervereinigung von Nord- und Südvietnam, und Hanoi wurde Hauptstadt der Sozialistischen Republik Vietnam. Heute ist die älteste Hauptstadt Südostasiens eine Stadt im Wandel. Die 1986 im Rahmen des Đổi mới eingeleiteten marktwirtschaftlichen Reformen haben auch im Straßenbild Spuren hinterlassen: Während laut Verfassung die Führung des Landes nach wie vor allein in den Händen der Kommunistischen Partei Vietnams liegt, prägen in den Straßen Hanois bunte Werbeplakate die Szenerie.

In 1945, after the Japanese occupation of World War II, Hồ Chí Minh proclaimed the Democratic Republic of Vietnam, and Hanoi was established as its capital. What followed were two long wars for hegemony in a divided country. It was not until 1975 that the fighting ended, North and South Vietnam were reunified, and Hanoi became the capital of the Socialist Republic of Vietnam. Today, Southeast Asia's oldest capital is a city in transition. The free-market reforms initiated in 1986 as part of the Đổi Mới policy have also left their mark on the streetscape: even though the constitution provides that leadership of the country is still solely in the hands of the Communist Party of Vietnam, the scenery in the streets of Hanoi is dominated by colorful advertising posters.

| **Hanoi in Zahlen** | Fläche: 3 345 km² | Bevölkerung: 8,1 Mio. (2019) |
| **Hanoi in numbers** | Area: 3,345 km² | Population: 8.1 million (2019) |

	Nationalversammlung		Schienen
	National Assembly building		Railway
	Städtische Bebauung		Wasserwege
	Urban building		Waterways
	Straßen		Grünanlagen
	Streets		Greens

Stadtgebiet Hanoi
Hanoi city area

Vorwort

Meinhard von Gerkan

Als wir 2007 den internationalen Wettbewerb für den Neubau der Nationalversammlung von Vietnam gewannen, waren von gmp in Hanoi bereits drei große öffentliche Projekte realisiert oder im Bau: das Nationale Kongresszentrum, das Innenministerium und das Hanoi Museum. Die Entscheidung der Jury fiel einstimmig, obgleich unser Entwurf keine symbolisch-repräsentativen Elemente enthielt und jedwede historisierende Anmutung vermied.

Bauherr und unmittelbarer Ansprechpartner für uns war das Bauministerium des Landes, und zuständig im Laufe der Planungszeit waren mehrere Vize-Bauminister. Einer von ihnen war keineswegs mit unserer Architekturauffassung einverstanden. Man dürfe nicht einfach modern bauen, hielt er uns entgegen und forderte uns auf, dem Gebäude einen traditionell vietnamesisch geprägten Ausdruck zu verleihen. Seine Vorstellung vermochte er mit wenigen Strichen grob zu skizzieren, die er uns als Vorlage an die Hand gab. Wir wollten jedoch keinesfalls irgendein Klischee vietnamesischer Kultur bedienen, wie es in Kitschprodukten entlang der vietnamesischen Straßen massenhaft verbreitet wird.

Denn ich vertrete grundsätzlich die Auffassung, dass die Bauten der Gegenwart einen Anspruch darauf haben, sich mit zeitgemäßen Konstruktionen und Baustoffen in heutiger Formensprache selbst zu behaupten. Jedes heute entworfene Gebäude ist ein zeitgeschichtlicher Beitrag, der durch seine Eigenständigkeit zugleich Abbild unserer Gesellschaft ist. Jede Generation hat das Recht, ja sogar die Pflicht, aus den jeweiligen Bedingungen der Gegenwart heraus ihren baugeschichtlichen Beitrag zu leisten. Tradierte architektonische Ausdrucksformen können dieser Pflicht ebenso wenig genügen, wie der Wiederaufbau historischer Gebäude nur Ausnahme bleiben kann. Das Berliner Schloss unter dem Namen Humboldt Forum als eine verfremdete Replik der Vergangenheit aufleben zu lassen, empfinde ich entsprechend als Armutszeugnis für die deutsche Baukultur. Nur eine mutige zeitgemäße Architektur kann markante Spuren hinterlassen.

Aber Architektur, wie ich sie verstehe – als Kunst in der sozialen Anwendung – entsteht im Dialog: Jede Wettbewerbsarbeit stellt eine geistige Gratwanderung zwischen den einengenden äußeren Bedingungen und den eigenen, teilweise entgegengesetzten Absichten dar. Die Grenze zwischen Sollen und Wollen ist im Dialog mit der Aufgabenstellung jeweils neu auszuloten. Dabei ist es

Meinhard von Gerkan (2. v. r.) mit Nikolaus Goetze (l.), Duc Tran Cong (2. v. l.) und Dirk Heller (r.)
Meinhard von Gerkan (second from right) with Nikolaus Goetze (left), Duc Tran Cong (second from left), and Dirk Heller (right)

Preface

In 2007, when we won the international competition for the new building for Vietnam's National Assembly, three large public projects had already been completed by gmp in Hanoi or were under construction there: the National Conference Center, the Ministry of the Interior, and the Hanoi Museum. The jury's decision was unanimous, even though our design was devoid of symbolic-representative elements and entirely avoided any historicizing imagery.

Our client and direct contact was the country's Ministry of Construction, and several Deputy Ministers of Construction were in charge over the course of the project's planning. One of them did not agree at all with our understanding of architecture. One must not simply build in a modern way, he countered, and called on us to give the building an appearance infused with traditional Vietnamese character. With a few strokes, he was able to roughly sketch out his idea, which he handed to us as a template. But we did not want to cater in any way to some cliché of Vietnamese culture of the sort that is disseminated en masse in kitsch products along Vietnamese streets.

For I am fundamentally of the opinion that the buildings of the present are entitled to assert themselves with contemporary structures and building materials in today's formal language. Every building designed today is a contribution to contemporary history that, thanks to its independence, is at the same time a reflection of our society. Every generation has the right, indeed the obligation, to make its own contribution to building history based on the prevailing conditions of the present. Traditional architectonic forms of expression cannot fulfill this obligation any more than the reconstruction of historical buildings can remain an exception. To resurrect the Berlin Palace under the name Humboldt Forum as an alienated replica of the past is, in my opinion, a sad commentary on German building culture. Only courageous contemporary architecture can make a distinctive mark.

But architecture as I understand it, as art applied in a social context, is created in dialog: every competition entry constitutes an intellectual balancing act between the constraining external conditions and one's own, sometimes opposing intentions. The boundary between what is requested and what one wants to achieve must be newly explored each time, in dialog with the formulated task. In doing so, it is essential that one neither blindly implements program demands nor proceeds too autocratically with only one's own goals in mind. In this way,

a dialog between the established notions of specialists and competitors' novel ideas unfolds anew with every competition. Entrenched values and professional bias are thereby continually called into question.

However, the expectations of the client, or rather of those who represent the client—that the parliament building should correspond to a traditional or supposedly traditional Vietnamese architecture—were in this case hindered by a specific building-cultural circumstance over and above our reservations as architects. For even though the debate about building with historical architectural forms is notoriously at least as pronounced in Europe as it is in Vietnam or even China, there is a crucial difference that acts there from the outset as an impediment to the choice that exists, at least theoretically, between past and present. In Europe, almost all the historical buildings that in some cases are reconstructed as replicas—such as the aforementioned Berlin Palace with its baroque facade and new architectural form inside—have a conformation in terms of size, number of stories, and structural order that fundamentally makes it possible to satisfy present-day use requirements. In Vietnam or China, by contrast, buildings are presently under construction whose immense dimensions have nothing at all in common with traditional small-scale architecture, which is why traditional attributes that are decoratively applied to a building's exterior or motifs reproduced on mirrored glass facades necessarily become caricatures. An architecture that utilizes pseudo-historicizing embellishments and decorative, superficial additions is only capable of producing facelessness.

With the Vietnamese National Assembly building, fate came to our aid. In the spring of 2008, the Foreign Minister of the Federal Republic of Germany at the time, Frank-Walter Steinmeier, visited Vietnam. I was among those who escorted him and asked permission to accompany him to an audience with the Prime Minister in order to obtain information at the highest level about the country's design expectations for their parliament building. Permission was granted, and in response to my question to the Prime Minister—of whether there was a single building in Vietnam in which the symbiosis of supposedly typical Vietnamese architecture with modern uses and a modern architectural guise has been successfully achieved—he replied in the negative. Nonetheless, because the minister considers us to be good architects, it is now also our task to solve this conondrum. We were assigned a team of numerous experts to assist us, consisting

wesentlich, weder Programmvorgaben unreflektiert umzusetzen noch allzu selbstherrlich nur von eigenen Zielsetzungen auszugehen. Auf diese Weise vollzieht sich bei jedem Wettbewerb aufs Neue ein Dialog zwischen den etablierten Vorstellungen von Fachspezialisten und neuen Ideen der Wettbewerber. Festgefahrene Wertvorstellungen und fachspezifische Befangenheit werden dadurch ständig infrage gestellt.

Den Vorstellungen des Bauherrn beziehungsweise der ihn vertretenden Personen, dass der Parlamentsbau einer traditionellen (oder vermeintlich traditionellen) vietnamesischen Architektur entsprechen sollte, stand in diesem Fall jedoch über unseren Vorbehalt als Architekten hinaus noch eine spezifische baukulturelle Bedingung entgegen. Denn auch wenn die Diskussion um das Bauen in historischen Bauformen in Europa bekanntermaßen mindestens so ausgeprägt ist wie in Vietnam oder auch in China, besteht ein wesentlicher Unterschied, der dort die zumindest theoretisch bestehende Wahlmöglichkeit zwischen Vergangenheit und Gegenwart von vornherein verstellt: Die historischen Bauten, die in Europa teilweise als Repliken wiederhergestellt werden – wie das schon genannte Berliner Schloss mit barocker Fassade und neuer Bauform im Inneren – weisen nahezu allesamt in Größe, Anzahl der Geschosse und struktureller Ordnung eine Form auf, die es grundsätzlich ermöglicht, heutige Nutzungsanforderungen zu erfüllen. In Vietnam oder China hingegen werden heute Bauten erstellt, deren immense Dimension mit der traditionellen kleinmaßstäblichen Architektur überhaupt nichts gemeinsam hat, weshalb traditionelle Attribute, die an der Fassade dekorativ angebracht werden, oder Motive, die in Spiegelglasfassaden nachgezeichnet werden, notwendigerweise zu einer Karikatur geraten. Eine Architektur, die mit pseudohistorisierenden Verbrämungen und dekorativen, vordergründigen Zutaten operiert, ist nur geeignet, Gesichtslosigkeit zu erzeugen.

Bei der Vietnamesischen Nationalversammlung kam uns in dieser Situation das Schicksal zur Hilfe. Im Frühjahr 2008 besuchte der damalige Außenminister der Bundesrepublik Deutschland, Frank-Walter Steinmeier, Vietnam. Ich gehörte zu seinen Begleitern und bat um die Erlaubnis, ihn zu einer Audienz beim Premierminister begleiten zu dürfen, um von höchster Stelle Informationen über die gestalterischen Erwartungen des Landes an sein Parlamentsgebäude zu erhalten. Dies wurde erlaubt und meine an den Premierminister gerichtete Frage, ob es in Vietnam ein einziges Gebäude gäbe, bei dem die Symbiose angeblich typisch vietnamesischer Architektur mit modernen Nutzungen und einer modernen Baugestalt zustande gebracht worden sei, verneinte er. Weil er uns jedoch für gute Architekten halte, sei es nunmehr auch unsere Aufgabe, dieses Problem zu lösen. Man stellte uns ein mehrköpfiges Expertenteam an die Seite, bestehend aus aktiven Professoren und Architekten. Wir begannen, zahllose Varianten des Parlamentsgebäudes zu erarbeiten, insbesondere Variationen seines gestalterischen Ausdrucks nach außen.

Mit dem Ziel, dem Bauwerk eine inhaltsbezogene Identität zu verleihen, die weder von funktioneller Eingleisigkeit noch von einem gestalterischen Dogma diktiert wird, haben wir uns dann, wie bereits bei vielen Entwürfen in der Vergangenheit, der Geometrie als Mittler zwischen Funktion und Form bedient. Die Gesetzmäßigkeit verschiedener geometrischer Elementarformen – ob Kreis, Quadrat, Dreieck oder Sechseck – dient dabei als ordnendes und strukturierendes Medium, durch das wir die Funktionen in eine räumliche und baukörperliche Form bringen. Das gilt für die große Gesamtform gleichermaßen wie für jedes Detail.

Für den Bau der Nationalversammlung mündete dies im Grundriss in einer Überlagerung von Kreis und Quadrat, räumlich gesehen die Durchdringung von Quader und Kegelstumpf. In den Ansichten besteht die geometrische Ordnung aus einer Struktur vertikaler Lisenen, die sich von unten nach oben verdichten. Mit dieser vorgelagerten Ebene und der Orientierung der Büro- und Sitzungsräume zu den ins Volumen eingeschnittenen Höfen wird vermieden, dass sich der Parlamentsbau wie ein x-beliebiges Bürogebäude präsentiert. Das Gebäude wird somit zu einer minimalisierten dreidimensionalen Grafik. Die innere Logik und klare Gesetzmäßigkeit geometrischer Strukturen bilden damit eine Analogie zu unserer funktionellen Maxime, die auf elementare Einfachheit ausgerichtet ist.

Es gelang uns mit diesem Konzept, die grundlegenden Vorbehalte der Experten im freundschaftlichen Gedankenaustausch zu zerstreuen. Entstanden ist im dialogischen Prozess schließlich ein von der ursprünglich geplanten Ausdrucksstruktur abweichender Entwurf. In der städtebaulichen Fernwirkung dominiert die geometrische Regelhaftigkeit, während auf den zweiten Blick, im kleineren Maßstab aus unmittelbarer Nähe betrachtet, die Fassaden differenzierter und ornamentierter erscheinen – das Ergebnis eines langwierigen und schwierigen interkulturellen Austauschs, bei dem sich geradezu beispielhaft meine oft wiederholte Grundhaltung zum dialogischen Charakter eines jeden Entwurfsprozesses manifestierte. Die von mir für notwendig erachtete Selbstbehauptung der Gegenwartsarchitektur in Form, Material, Konstruktion und auch Dimension vermochte auf diese Weise sehr wohl die vielfältigen spezifischen Bedingungen zu respektieren und in eine Entwurfslösung mit charaktervoller Qualität zu integrieren.

of active professors and architects. We began to develop countless variants of the parliament building, especially variations of its outward artistic manifestation.

With the goal of giving the building an identity, related to its intrinsic functions, an identity dictated neither by functional single-mindedness nor by a design dogma, we then availed ourselves of geometry as an intermediary between function and form, as we have done for many designs in the past. The regularity of various geometric elementary forms—whether circle, square, triangle, or hexagon—serves as an ordering and structuring medium through which we bring the functions into a spatial and architectural form. This pertains in equal measure to the large form as a whole and to the smallest detail.

For the National Assembly building, this culminated in plan in a superimposition of circle and square, and spatially in an interpenetration of cuboid and truncated cone. On the elevations, the geometric arrangement consists of a pattern of vertical pilaster strips that become denser toward the top. Setting this layer in front and orienting the office and conference rooms to the courtyards that are cut into the volume avoids a situation in which the parliament has the appearance of a random office building. Hence the structure becomes a minimalized three-dimensional graphic. The inner logic and clear regularity of geometric structures thus form an analogy to our functional maxim of elementary simplicity.

This concept enabled us to dispel the fundamental reservations of the experts in a friendly exchange of ideas. Ultimately, the process of dialog resulted in a design that deviated from the originally envisaged expressive form. The building's geometric regularity dominates the image seen from afar within the urban context, while a second glance, when viewed at closer range and focusing at smaller scale, reveals facades that appear more differentiated and ornamented—the result of a protracted and difficult intercultural interchange in which my oft-repeated basic stance toward the dialogical character of every design process manifested itself in nothing less than an exemplary manner. The self-assertion of contemporary architecture in form, material, construction, and also dimension, which I deem necessary, was in this way very well able to respect the numerous specific conditions and to integrate them into a design solution with a quality full of character.

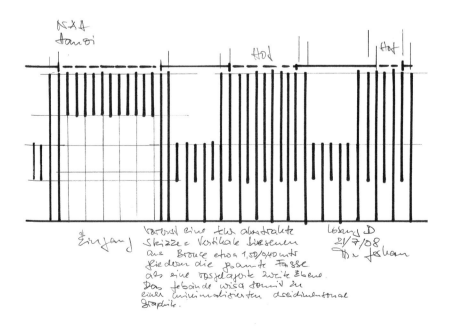

Entwurfsskizze von Meinhard von Gerkan
Design sketch by Meinhard von Gerkan

Mut zum Fortschritt – Bewusstsein für Tradition

Nikolaus Goetze

In den zurückliegenden fünfeinhalb Jahrzehnten haben wir bei gmp weltweit fast 500 Projekte, vom Einfamilienhaus über den Flughafen bis zur Planung einer ganzen Stadt (Lingang New City, heute Nanhui New City), realisiert – und doch war der Bau der Vietnamesischen Nationalversammlung in Hanoi für uns ein Novum, denn es ist das erste Parlamentsgebäude von gmp. Fast zwanzig Jahre nahm die Verwirklichung des Projekts in Anspruch – ein Zeitraum, in dem Vietnam so dynamisch vorangeschritten ist wie nur wenige andere Länder weltweit.

In welchem Tempo sich der heutige „Tigerstaat" entwickelt hat, lässt sich anhand des Verkehrs veranschaulichen: Ende der 1990er-Jahre prägten noch Millionen von Radfahrerinnen und Radfahrern das Straßenbild, motorisierte Zweiräder oder gar Autos gab es damals kaum. Heute ist es genau umgekehrt. Doch nicht nur die Mobilität in Vietnam, auch die Gesellschaft insgesamt hat sich eklatant verändert. Aus einem armen Arbeiter- und Bauernstaat ist ein moderner, noch immer sozialistisch geprägter und dennoch facettenreicher Vielvölkerstaat mit 54 anerkannten Minderheiten geworden, dessen vergleichsweise junge Bevölkerung vor allem in den großen Städten zunehmend an den Segnungen, allerdings auch an den Herausforderungen der Globalisierung teilhat.

Für mich war das Bauen in Vietnam von Anfang an eine sehr emotionale Angelegenheit. Im Unterschied etwa zu China mit seinen über 1,4 Milliarden Menschen und seinen Riesenstädten ist Vietnam hinsichtlich der Landesfläche, der Bevölkerungsgröße und auch der Stadtstrukturen durchaus mit den großen europäischen Ländern vergleichbar. Und bei aller Lust am Fortschritt spielen in Vietnam das Bewusstsein für Tradition und die eigene Kultur – von der Musik bis zur Kulinarik – eine wichtige Rolle.

Die vom staatlichen Auftraggeber gewünschte Verortung der Tradition Vietnams und unseren architektonischen Anspruch miteinander in Einklang zu bringen – darin bestand die besondere Herausforderung bei der Planung eines Parlamentsgebäudes in Hanoi, das die Kultur des Landes widerspiegeln und zugleich seine Modernität zum Ausdruck bringen sollte. Unsere ersten Entwürfe im Rahmen eines städtebaulichen Wettbewerbs reichen zurück bis ins Jahr 1998. In dieser Zeit für einen staatlichen Auftraggeber in Vietnam zu planen,

war ein schwieriges Unterfangen. Wir sind gewissermaßen ins kalte Wasser gesprungen, denn wir hatten noch keine Mitarbeiterinnen und Mitarbeiter vor Ort und auch noch kein Partnerbüro, wir mussten also zunächst eigene Strukturen aufbauen. Immerhin konnten wir von den früheren, teils langjährigen Aufenthalten einiger unserer vietnamesischen Kontaktleute in der DDR profitieren.

Die Aufgabe damals lautete, im zentralen, historisch bedeutsamen Viertel Ba Đình – mit dem Präsidentenpalast aus französischer Kolonialzeit und dem von sowjetischen Architekten geplanten Hồ Chí Minh-Mausoleum in unmittelbarer Nachbarschaft – ein Regierungsgebäude mit Kongresszentrum zu planen. Wir haben damals zwei Varianten entwickelt: die erste mit einem kompakten Gebäude und die zweite (von uns präferierte) mit einem zweigeteilten Gebäude beiderseits der west-östlichen Achse [1], die das Mausoleum mit dem Monument der Gefallenen verbindet. Den Plänen zufolge wäre in einem ersten Bauabschnitt das Kongresszentrum mit nahezu quadratischem Kopfbau neben dem seinerzeit noch existierenden historischen Gebäude der Nationalversammlung, der Ba Đình Hall, entstanden, in einem zweiten Bauabschnitt dann das neue Parlamentsgebäude mit einem runden Kopfbau. Ein öffentlicher Platz hätte die beiden einander gegenüberliegenden Gebäude miteinander verbunden.

Unsere Entwürfe wurden zunächst nicht weiterverfolgt; erst fünf Jahre später wurden wir, zusammen mit rund zehn weiteren teilnehmenden Büros, zu einem Architekturwettbewerb eingeladen. Die Prämisse war jetzt, das gesamte Bauvolumen auf einem Grundstück unterzubringen. Für unseren Entwurf eines kompakten, diesmal west-östlich ausgerichteten Baukörpers nördlich der Ba Đình Hall erhielten wir 2003 den ersten Preis [2›]. Die Grundrisse der beiden Hauptbaukörper – des Abgeordnetensaals und des Kongresssaals – basierten auf den Elementarformen von Kreis und Quadrat. Der kreisförmige Versammlungssaal mit der radialen Anordnung der Bestuhlung sollte den fast 500 Abgeordneten, die hier in der Regel zweimal im Jahr für je sechs Wochen zusammentreten, beste Sicht- und optimale akustische Bedingungen ermöglichen. Der kegelstumpfförmige Körper des Saals mit nach außen geneigten Wänden sollte von einer großen Eingangshalle mit freiem Blick auf den Ba Đình-Platz und zum gegenüberliegenden Mausoleum gerahmt werden.

Courage to Embrace Progress— Awareness of Tradition

Over the past five and a half decades, we at gmp have realized nearly 500 projects around the world, from single-family houses to airports to the master planning for an entire city (Lingang New City, now Nanhui New City)—yet the building for the Vietnamese National Assembly in Hanoi was unique, as it is the first parliament building by gmp. Almost twenty years were needed to bring the project to fruition—a timespan in which Vietnam has made more dynamic progress than most other countries in the world.

The speed at which today's "Asian Tiger" has advanced can be illustrated by how its transport has developed: at the end of the 1990s, the streetscape was still dominated by millions of cyclists; back then, there were hardly any motorized two-wheeled vehicles or even cars. Today it is exactly the opposite. But not only has mobility in Vietnam changed dramatically, so has society as a whole. An impoverished country of workers and farmers has become a modern, multiethnic state, with fifty-four recognized minorities, that remains socialist in character despite being multifaceted, and whose comparatively young population increasingly shares in the blessings as well as the challenges of globalization, especially in the large cities.

For me, building in Vietnam was a very emotional affair from the outset. In contrast to China, for example, with its more than 1.4 billion people and its megacities, Vietnam is quite comparable to the large European countries in terms of land area, population size, and also urban structures. And despite all the passion for progress, an awareness of tradition and of the country's own culture—from music to cuisine—plays an important role in Vietnam.

Reconciling the rooted embodiment of Vietnam's tradition, as desired by the state client, with our own architectural aspirations—therein lay the exceptional challenge in designing a parliament building in Hanoi that was to reflect the culture of the country and at the same time give expression to its modernity. Our first designs, done for an urban planning competition, date back to 1998. Working as architects for a state client in Vietnam during that time was a difficult undertaking. We plunged in at the deep end, so to speak, because we did not yet have any locally based staff and we also did not have a partner firm, so first we had to establish an organization of our own. At least we were able to

benefit from the experiences gathered by some of our Vietnamese contacts during their earlier stays in the GDR, some of which had lasted many years.

The task at that time was to design a government building with a conference center in the central, historically significant district of Ba Đình—with its presidential palace dating from French colonial times and the Hồ Chí Minh mausoleum, designed by Soviet architects, in immediate proximity.

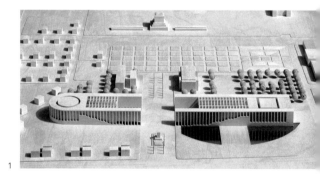

1

We developed two variants that differed at urban scale: the first had a compact building, and the second (our preference) had a building divided into two parts on either side of the east-west axis [1] that runs between the mausoleum and the Bắc Sơn Monument to Heroic Martyrs. According to the plans, the first phase of construction would have been the conference center to the north, with an almost square main building next to the historical building of the National Assembly, Ba Đình Hall (which was still existant at that time), and the second phase would have been the new parliament building with a round main building. A public square would have connected the two buildings on opposite sides.

Initially our designs were not pursued any further, and not until five years later were we invited to participate in an architectural competition together with about ten other participants. The premise at that point was to accommodate the entire volume of construction on one plot of land. This time our design for a compact building north of Ba Đình Hall was oriented east-west, and in 2003 we were awarded first prize [2›].

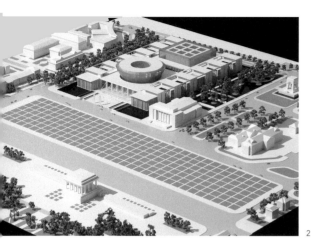

2

Zwei Gebäuderiegel mit Konferenz- und Verwaltungs-räumen für den gesamten Komplex sollten den Abge-ordnetensaal, die Eingangshalle und den als Kubus gestalteten Kongresssaal seitlich fassen.

Da 2004, kurz nach dem Beginn der Bauarbeiten, auf dem Bauplatz, einem Teil des Areals des Kaiserpalas-tes, über tausend Jahre alte archäologische Funde frei-gelegt wurden (die heute im Ausstellungsbereich im Untergeschoss der Nationalversammlung ausgestellt sind), wurde der Bau mit sofortiger Wirkung gestoppt. Weil aber für das Jahr 2006 in Hanoi ein Treffen der Re-gierungschefs der APEC-Staaten geplant war, für das noch kein geeignetes Kongresszentrum zur Verfügung stand, bekamen wir kurzfristig den Direktauftrag, vier unabhängige Entwürfe für ein reines Kongresszentrum an einem anderen Ort, eingebettet in eine Parkland-schaft westlich der Innenstadt, zu entwickeln. Wie bei einem beschränkten Wettbewerb erarbeiteten bei uns im Büro vier Teams unabhängig voneinander Entwürfe für das National Convention Center, von denen einer – mit einer gewellten Dachstruktur [3], die sich über dem großen Kongresssaal zu großer Höhe aufschwingt – ausgewählt und in einer Rekordzeit von zwei Jahren geplant und gebaut wurde. In dieser Zeit eröffneten wir gemeinsam mit unseren Projektpartnern von Inros Lackner eine Büroniederlassung in Hanoi, was sich später bei Planung und Bau der Nationalversammlung und auch bei allen nachfolgenden Projekten in Viet-nam sehr bewährt hat. Im Falle der Nationalversamm-lung hat es die Zusammenarbeit mit der staatlichen Bauherrschaft und mit den lokalen Partnerbüros deut-lich erleichtert.

Im Jahr 2007 wurde ein neuer Architekturwettbewerb ausgeschrieben, nun für ein reines Parlamentsgebäu-de am Ba Đình-Platz. Diese Entscheidung erwies sich letztlich als Glücksfall, denn die Verkehrsbelastung in der unmittelbaren Umgebung des Gebäudes hätte deutlich zugenommen, wenn dort zusätzlich ein Kon-gresszentrum entstanden wäre. Standort der künftigen Vietnamesischen Nationalversammlung sollte nun das Grundstück der inzwischen zum Abriss bestimmten Ba Đình Hall sein, gegenüber dem Außenministerium und schräg gegenüber dem Mausoleum. An dem Wettbewerb nahmen insgesamt 17 Architekturbüros teil, und wir erhielten zum zweiten Mal den ersten Preis.

Beim Entwurf für die Nationalversammlung griffen wir auf die archetypische Geometrie des vier Jahre zuvor ausgearbeiteten Entwurfs für ein Parlament mit inte-griertem Kongresszentrum zurück: Der kegelstumpf-förmige Abgeordnetensaal wächst gewissermaßen aus dem kompakten kubischen Baukörper heraus [4], des-sen drei oberste Geschosse durch hofartige, begrünte Einschnitte mit der umgebenden Kulturlandschaft buchstäblich verzahnt sind. Eine in Wuchshöhe und Blütezeit durchkomponierte Vegetation holt die Natur bildlich in das Gebäude hinein. Mit seiner Fassade aus Jadeglas ist der Plenarsaal schon von weitem über dem dichten Häusermeer der Altstadt von Hanoi mit der Zitadelle Thăng Long sichtbar. Materialität und Farbkanon der Fassade, das grüne Glas und der beige-farbene Naturstein, verweisen auf die im Stadtbild von Hanoi vielfach vertretene Farbkombination aus Grün und Gelb. Lisenen aus fein gearbeitetem und gleich-mäßig strukturiertem Granit [5›], die sich in vertikaler Anordnung nach oben hin immer weiter verdichten, gliedern die Fassade. Im Erdgeschoss und im Bereich des VIP-Eingangs im Süden auch im zweiten Ober-geschoss sind zwischen den Granitstreifen ornamen-tierte bronzefarbene Metallelemente eingefügt, die der Verschattung und als Sichtschutz dienen. Auch die Stirnseiten der weit auskragenden metallenen Vor-dächer über dem VIP- und auch über dem Hauptein-gang für Abgeordnete und Besucherinnen und Besu-cher im Westen sind durch Ornamente geprägt; sie stellen einen stilisierten Phönix dar, eines der vier Fabeltiere Vietnams und ein Symbol für Schönheit und Erfolg.

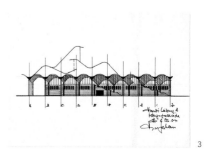

3

The plans for the two main parts of the building—the hall of representatives and the conference hall—were based on the elementary shapes of circle and square. The circular assembly chamber, with its radial seating configuration, was designed to provide the best possible visual and acoustic conditions for the nearly 500 parliamentary representatives, who usually meet here twice a year for six-week periods. The truncated cone-shape of the hall, with its outward sloping walls, was to be visually framed by a large entrance hall with an unobstructed view of Ba Đình Square and the mausoleum opposite. Two wings with conference and administrative rooms for the entire complex were to embrace the sides of the hall of representatives, the entrance hall, and the cube-shaped conference hall.

In 2004, shortly after construction work had begun on the building site—part of the former grounds of the imperial palace—archaeological finds dating back more than a thousand years (which are now on display in the basement exhibition area of the National Assembly) were uncovered, prompting construction to be halted with immediate effect. However, because a meeting of the heads of government of the APEC states was planned for 2006 in Hanoi, for which no suitable congress center was yet available and there was insufficient time for a competition, we were given the direct commission at short notice to develop four separate designs for a stand-alone conference center on a different site, nestled in a park landscape to the west of the city center. Just like in a restricted competition, four teams in our office worked independently of one another to develop designs for the National Convention Center, and one of these schemes—with an undulating roof structure [3] that soars up high above the large convention hall—was selected and then planned and built in a record time of two years. During this time, we and our project partners from Inros Lackner opened a joint branch office in Hanoi—which later proved its worth, not only as we were planning and constructing the National Assembly building but also in all our subsequent projects in Vietnam. In the case of the National Assembly building, this greatly facilitated our coordination efforts with the state client and our local partner firms.

In 2007 a new architectural competition was held, this time for a stand-alone parliament building on Ba Đình Square. This decision ultimately proved to be a stroke of luck, because traffic congestion in the immediate vicinity of the building would have increased significantly if a conference center had also been constructed there. The future Vietnamese National Assembly building was now to be located opposite the Ministry of Foreign Affairs and diagonally across from the mausoleum, on the site of Ba Đình Hall, which had meanwhile been scheduled for demolition. A total of seventeen architectural firms took part in the competition, and we were awarded first prize for the second time.

4

For the design of the National Assembly building, we drew on the archetypal geometry of the design for a parliament building with an integrated conference center that we had developed four years earlier: the truncated cone-shaped hall of representatives grows, as it were, out of the compact, cube-like form [4], whose three uppermost stories are literally intertwined with the surrounding cultural landscape by courtyard-like, planted recesses. Vegetation, meticulously composed in terms of growth height and flowering time, metaphorically brings nature into the building. With its facade of jade-colored glass, the plenary hall is visible from afar above the dense sea of houses in the Old Quarter of Hanoi, home of Thăng Long citadel. The palette of materials and colors of the facade, the green glass and the beige-colored natural stone, makes reference to the color combination green-yellow, which is widely on display in Hanoi's cityscape. Pilaster strips of finely crafted and evenly patterned granite [5 ›], whose vertical arrangement becomes increasingly dense toward the top, articulate the facade. On the ground floor, ornamented bronze-colored metal elements provide shade and serve as visual screening for the public areas located there. Ornamentation also distinguishes the fascias of the deeply cantilevered metal canopies above both the VIP entrance and the main entrance on the west side, for parliamentary delegates and visitors alike; the embellishment portrays a stylized phoenix, one of the four mythical creatures of Vietnam, as a symbol of beauty and success.

Diese Mehrschichtigkeit der Fassade, die Details, die sich dem Betrachter erst beim genaueren Hinsehen offenbaren – dieser Aspekt spielt in der Architektur in Vietnam eine wichtige Rolle. Diese Erkenntnis verdanken wir dem Gremium aus sechs vietnamesischen Architekturexperten (von denen ein Teil in Weimar studiert hatte), mit denen wir uns bei der Planung berieten. Neben diesem Gremium hatte das Projektmanagement-Board des Bauministeriums eine wichtige Vermittlerfunktion zwischen der vietnamesischen Regierung als Auftraggeberin und uns Architekten. Es bestand aus bis zu 100 Mitgliedern und war für die Planung, Ausschreibung, Vergabe und Bauleitung zuständig. Wir haben die außergewöhnlich enge und respektvolle Zusammenarbeit mit einer „Bauherrschaft zum Anfassen" im Rahmen dieses Projekts sehr zu schätzen gelernt, ebenso wie die Einstellung, sowohl auf „das große Ganze" im Sinne einer repräsentativen Erscheinung als auch auf die harmonische Addition vieler einzelner Elemente zu achten.

5

Herzstück der Nationalversammlung ist der von einem großen Foyer umgebene Plenarsaal mit einem Durchmesser von 51 Metern, der aus Gründen der Erdbebensicherheit vom übrigen Gebäude konstruktiv getrennt ist und auf acht im Foyer sichtbaren Stahlbetonstützen lagert. Der Saal, der den rund 500 Abgeordneten aus den fünf Städten und 58 Provinzen Vietnams und auf der Galerie bis zu 340 Besucherinnen und Besuchern Platz bietet, ist mit Holz ausgekleidet. Die Sitzreihen der Abgeordneten sind, ebenso wie die halbkreisförmige Zuschauergalerie, kreissegmentförmig auf das zentrale Podium an der östlichen Stirnseite ausgerichtet. Blickfang des Saals ist die bis in eine Höhe von 26 Metern reichende, flache Kuppeldecke, die insgesamt 950 Quadratmeter misst. Sie setzt sich aus 4500 LEDs und 9400 satinierten Glasscheiben zusammen, die in 34 Ringen angeordnet sind.

Hinter der Kuppeldecke verbirgt sich die Dachkonstruktion aus radial angeordneten Stahlträgern, die auf Stahlbetonkonsolen an der Außenwand lagern; zwei Stahlringe steifen die Konstruktion im Inneren aus[6]. Die Felder zwischen den Stahlträgern sind mit Stahlbetonfertigteilen ausgefacht. Auch die Bodenplatte des Plenarsaals ist eine Stahlbetonkonstruktion, die wie ein Speichenrad aufgebaut ist: Acht radial angeordnete Trägerpaare verbinden den Außenring mit einem Innenring von 10 Metern Durchmesser.

Die Vietnamesische Nationalversammlung fand bereits unmittelbar nach ihrer Fertigstellung als ikonischer Repräsentationsbau der Sozialistischen Republik Vietnam Anerkennung. Während bei dem benachbarten Präsidentenpalast aus der französischen Kolonialzeit und dem Mausoleum als Manifestation sowjetischen Bauens die fremden Einflüsse noch deutlich wahrgenommen wurden, spielt dies heute allenfalls eine untergeordnete Rolle. Die Tatsache, dass Architektur, Statik und Haustechnikplanung aus deutschen Büros stammten und dass überwiegend Ausbauelemente von Firmen aus Deutschland, Spanien, Korea und Japan verwendet wurden, ist heute genauso selbstverständlich wie etwa der Umstand, dass der Berliner Reichstag von einem britischen Architekten umgebaut wurde. Eine besondere Anerkennung für unsere Leistung bedeutete der Vietnamesische Nationalpreis für Architektur, mit dem der Bau der Vietnamesischen Nationalversammlung 2015 ausgezeichnet wurde.

6

This multilayered aspect of the facade—with details that only reveal themselves to the observer upon closer inspection—plays an important role in architecture in Vietnam. We owe this insight to the committee of six Vietnamese architectural experts (some of whom had studied in Weimar) with whom we consulted during the planning process. In addition to that committee, the Ministry of Construction's project management board played an important role as an intermediary between the Vietnamese government as client and us as architects. It consisted of up to 100 members and was responsible for the planning, calls for bids, contract awarding, and construction supervision. Over the course of this project, we came to greatly appreciate the exceptionally close and respectful collaboration with an "approachable client"—as well as the attitude of paying attention to "the big picture," both in the sense of creating an impactful appearance and in the harmonious integration of many individual elements.

The heart of the National Assembly building is the plenary hall, which is surrounded by an expansive lobby and has a diameter of 51 meters. To ensure earthquake safety, it is structurally separated from the rest of the building and bears on eight reinforced concrete columns that are prominently visible in the lobby. The hall, which seats some 500 delegates from Vietnam's five cities and 58 provinces on the floor and up to 340 visitors in the gallery, is paneled with wood. The rows of seats for the delegates, as well as the semicircular spectator gallery, are arranged as circular segments that face the central podium on the eastern side. The eye-catcher of the hall is its shallow-domed ceiling, which reaches a height of 26 meters and measures a total of 950 square meters. It is composed of 4,500 LEDs and 9,400 satin-finish glass panels arrayed in 34 rings.

The domed ceiling conceals the roof structure of radial steel girders bearing on reinforced concrete brackets on the exterior wall; two steel rings stiffen the structure inside [6]. The bays between the steel girders are infilled with elements of precast reinforced concrete. The floor slab of the plenary hall is also a reinforced concrete structure configured like a spoked wheel: eight radially disposed pairs of beams connect the outer ring with an inner ring measuring 10 meters in diameter.

Immediately after its completion, the Vietnamese National Assembly building was recognized as an iconic prestigious building representative of the Socialist Republic of Vietnam. Whereas foreign influences were still clearly visible in the nearby presidential palace from the French colonial period and the mausoleum, which is a manifestation of Soviet construction, at most such influences play a subordinate role these days. Today, the fact that the building was planned by German architects, structural engineers, and building services engineers and the fit-out elements were supplied chiefly by companies from Germany, Spain, Korea, and Japan goes as much without saying as does, for example, the fact that the Reichstag in Berlin was transformed by a British architect. As a special recognition of our achievement, the Vietnamese National Architecture Award was presented to the Vietnamese National Assembly building in 2015.

7

Die Geschichte der modernen Architektur in Vietnam

Trương Ngọc Lân

In fast allen südostasiatischen Ländern fand die Verbreitung moderner Architekturstile unter Einfluss westlicher Kultur statt. In Vietnam war der Prozess dieser Einflussnahme nie einfach, da er eng mit der Kolonialisierung und den daraus erwachsenden ideologischen Konflikten verbunden war. Daher hat sich die moderne Architektur in Vietnam nicht harmonisch entwickelt, und die Berufspraxis vietnamesischer Architekten war das gesamte vergangene Jahrhundert hindurch von politischen und ideologischen Auseinandersetzungen sowie von der Suche nach einer nationalen Identität geprägt.

DIE KOLONIALE VERGANGENHEIT

Mit der Landung französischer Truppen in Đà Nẵng 1858 und der Eroberung von Saigon 1859 begann die Kolonialisierung Indochinas. Zu Beginn des 20. Jahrhunderts gab die etablierte intellektuelle Elite des Landes die traditionelle konfuzianische Bildung allmählich zugunsten westlicher Werte auf. Um innerhalb der einheimischen Bevölkerung eine Schicht zu schaffen, die sich für die Arbeit im Verwaltungsapparat eignet, gründeten die Franzosen Bildungseinrichtungen. Der Unterricht fand in französischer Sprache statt, war eurozentrisch ausgerichtet und hatte die zunehmende Verbreitung der westlichen Kultur in Vietnam zur Folge.

Die Geburtsstunde der modernen Architektur in Vietnam schlägt um das Jahr 1925 mit der Gründung der École supérieure des beaux-arts de l'Indochine (EBAI) in Hanoi, der heutigen Universität der Schönen Künste Vietnams. Ein Jahr später entstand die Fakultät für Architektur. Zur gleichen Zeit setzte die Verwaltung ihr zweites koloniales Erschließungsprogramm für Indochina um, im Rahmen dessen viele neue Büros und Gebäude für den Handel sowie Wohnhäuser entstanden. Zudem fanden neue Materialien wie Beton und Stahl und mit ihnen auch neue Architekturströmungen Verbreitung. Die beliebtesten Stilrichtungen waren Art nouveau und Art déco.

Der Art nouveau erreichte Vietnam schon sehr früh; er fand sich zunächst nur in Details und einzelnen Gebäudeteilen, sollte aber dennoch prototypisch für spätere Entwicklungen der Architektur in Vietnam werden. Vor 1920 wurden bei einigen großen Bauten wie dem Opernhaus in Hanoi (1911) und dem Palais du Résident Supérieur du Tonkin (1917) für die Überdachung der Eingangsbereiche bereits Konstruktionen aus Metall und Glas nach dem Vorbild des europäischen Art nouveau gestaltet.

Das erste Bauwerk des Art déco in Hanoi war das Gebäude der l'Imprimerie d'Extrême-Orient (1929) [1]. In den 1930er-Jahren kam der Art déco dann von Hanoi bis Saigon in Mode. [**2** Hauptniederlassung der Indochina-Bank in Hanoi (1932) | **3** Sommerpalast von Kaiser Bảo Đại in Đà Lạt (1938)]

Vor 1945 bot sich den vietnamesischen Architekten wenig Gelegenheit zur Entwicklung eines eigenen Stils. Denn eine unabhängige berufliche Praxis war kaum möglich, und die Mehrheit der einheimischen Architekten fungierte als Helfer französischer Architekten. Nur wenige eröffneten eigene Büros, sie erhielten zudem nur kleine Aufträge, hauptsächlich Villen für die vietnamesische Oberschicht. Als „Bürger zweiter Klasse" und in Anbetracht der Lage ihres Landes engagierten sich daher viele von ihnen in Widerstandsbewegungen, die für die Unabhängigkeit Vietnams kämpften. Auch in der Ergründung der Identität des eigenen Volkes in der Gestaltung drückte sich Widerstand gegen die Kolonialmacht aus, Beispiele sind das Werk von Architekten wie Nguyễn Cao Luyện, Hoàng Như Tiếp oder Nguyễn Gia Đức.

1

2

The History of Modern Vietnamese Architecture

In almost all Southeast Asian countries, the propagation of modern architectural styles took place under the influence of Western culture. In Vietnam, this process of merging cultures was never easy because it was closely associated with colonization and the resulting ideological conflicts. For this reason, modern architecture in Vietnam has not developed harmoniously and the professional activity of Vietnamese architects was marked throughout the past century by political and ideological disputes and the search for a national identity.

THE COLONIAL PAST

The colonization of Indochina began with the landing of French troops in Đà Nẵng in 1858 and the conquest of Saigon in 1859. At the beginning of the twentieth century, the established intellectual elite of the country began to opt for Western values instead of the traditional Confucian education. In order to create a class of people within the local population who were suitable for work in public administration, the French founded educational establishments. Lessons were held in the French language; the curriculum was based on European values and resulted in Western culture becoming increasingly popular.

The birth of modern architecture in Vietnam took place in 1925 with the foundation of the École Supérieure des Beaux-Arts de l'Indochine (EBAI) in Hanoi, today the Vietnam University of Fine Arts. One year later, the Faculty of Architecture was created. At the same time, the administration implemented its second colonial development program for Indochina, which involved many new offices and commercial buildings, as well as houses. In addition, new materials such as concrete and steel became more widely used, which also led to new architectural trends. The most favored styles were Art Nouveau and Art Deco.

The Art Nouveau style reached Vietnam at a very early stage; at first it was only prominent in details and parts of buildings, but it nevertheless was the forerunner of later developments in Vietnam's architecture. Prior to 1920, some large buildings, such as the Opera House in Hanoi (1911) and the Palais du Résident Supérieur du Tonkin (1917), already featured metal and glass constructions in the style of the European Art Nouveau for the roofs over the entrance areas.

The first Art Deco building in Hanoi was that of the Imprimerie d'Extrême-Orient (1929) [1]. In the 1930s, Art Deco then became popular from Hanoi to Saigon. [2 Bank of Indochina Headquarter (1932) | 3 Summer Palace of Emperor Bảo Đại in Đà Lạt (1938)]

Prior to 1945, there was little opportunity for Vietnamese architects to develop their own style. This was because independent professional practice was almost impossible and the majority of domestic architects worked as assistants to their French counterparts. Very few opened their own practice; in addition, they only received small commissions, mainly for villas for the Vietnamese upper class. As "second-class citizens" and in view of the situation in their country, many therefore took part in resistance movements that fought for Vietnam's independence. The resistance against the colonial power also found expression in the search for identity in terms of design; examples are the oeuvre of architects such as Nguyễn Cao Luyện, Hoàng Như Tiếp, and Nguyễn Gia Đức.

THE FIGHT FOR INDEPENDENCE, 1945–1954

On September 2, 1945, Hồ Chí Minh proclaimed the independence of the Democratic Republic of Vietnam. However, the French soon returned after 1946. In consequence, many Vietnamese architects left the cities and

3

DER KAMPF UM DIE UNABHÄNGIGKEIT, 1945–1954

Am 2. September 1945 proklamierte Hồ Chí Minh die Unabhängigkeit der Demokratischen Republik Vietnam. Die Franzosen kehrten jedoch nach 1946 schnell zurück. Viele vietnamesische Architekten verließen daraufhin die Städte und schlossen sich dem Widerstand an, einige blieben aber auch in der Hoffnung auf berufliche Perspektiven. Nur sehr wenige Bauten von nennenswert künstlerischem Wert entstanden in dieser Zeit, denn der Krieg verursachte einen Rückgang der Bautätigkeit. In den Städten war der Art déco weiterhin der vorherrschende Stil. Jene Architekten, die Hồ Chí Minh gefolgt waren, arbeiteten mit stark eingeschränkten Ressourcen in den Wäldern. Dort schufen sie einen neuen Stil: Da weder Maschinen noch Facharbeiter verfügbar waren, wurde mit Arbeitskräften vor Ort und in Handarbeit mit vorhandenen Materialien wie Bambus, Lehm oder Fächerpalmwedeln gebaut. Viele große Bauten wurden zur Unterstützung der Widerstandskämpfer errichtet, wie die von Hoàng Như Tiếp 1950 gestaltete Versammlungsstätte für den zweiten Kongress der kommunistischen Partei. Dieses Bauwerk wurde komplett aus Bambus errichtet und war über 10 Meter hoch. Es bot ausreichend Platz für mehrere hundert Teilnehmer. Seine einfache Gestaltung mit einer eleganten Tragstruktur und die Bambusfassade lassen es wie einen Vorläufer der *Green Architecture* Anfang des 21. Jahrhunderts erscheinen.

DIE GETEILTE ARCHITEKTUR, 1954–1975

Nach neun Jahren Kampf gegen die französischen Besatzungstruppen, der schließlich in deren Abzug nach der Schlacht von Điện Biên Phủ endete, kehrte noch immer kein Frieden ein. Das Land wurde in zwei Teile mit zwei konträren Ideologien geteilt. Der Kampf um das Selbstbestimmungsrecht des Volkes, die Vereinigung des Landes und das Ende äußerer Einmischungen beherrschte das politische Denken vieler Vietnamesen und auch das der Architekten in beiden Systemen. Daher bestimmte die Suche nach modernen Lösungen mit nationalem Charakter die vietnamesische Architektur jener Zeit.

In Südvietnam stellten die Marktwirtschaft, die schnell voranschreitende Verstädterung und der unausweichliche Kontakt mit westlicher Kultur und Technik die Weichen für eine vielfältigere Entwicklung architektonischer Stile und Formen, als dies im Norden möglich war. Importierte Materialien wie Zement, Glas und Stahl waren im Bauwesen verbreitet und boten eine Fülle von Gestaltungsmöglichkeiten.

Einflüsse aus dem In- und Ausland gab es auch in der Architekturausbildung. Im Süden wurde der Kolonialstil zu einem großen Teil durch den International Style abgelöst. Doch auch hier überwog der Versuch, Elemente in die Gestaltung einzubinden, die dem tropischen Klima vor Ort gerecht wurden, wie im Fall des Unabhängigkeitspalastes in Saigon (1962) [4] von Ngô Viết Thụ. Die einfache Gesamtfigur des Bauwerks mit seinen kubischen Formen entspricht dem International Style. Durch breite Korridore um die Arbeitsräume und einen großen Innenhof für den Wohnbereich des Präsidenten ist für Verschattung und Kühlung gesorgt. Sowohl das System der Brise Soleil, das an Bambus und Fenstergitter aus der vietnamesischen Bautradition erinnert, als auch die Ornamentik gehen auf die landestypische Ästhetik zurück. Auch im Fall der Nationalbibliothek von Saigon (1968) [5] von Nguyễn Hữu Thiện manifestiert sich ein nationaler Charakter in der Gestaltung des Sonnenschutzes in Anlehnung an traditionelle Bauformen. So wirkt die Bibliothek keineswegs wie ein Fremdkörper, auch wenn sie vollständig aus Beton gebaut ist und durch ihre strenge, orthogonale Geometrie auffällt.

Gebäude wie die in Stahlbeton ausgeführte Vĩnh Nghiêm-Pagode (1971) [6] und die Versammlungshalle der Universität Cần Thơ drücken in ihrer Formensprache ebenfalls einen nationalen Charakter aus. Im Norden Vietnams schritt die urbane Entwicklung während des Krieges nur sehr langsam voran. Wirtschaft und Politik waren zentralisiert, Aufträge gab es nur seitens der Regierung – private Auftraggeber existierten nicht –, und es fand nur wenig Austausch mit westlicher Kultur statt, weshalb vor 1975 die Architektur im Norden formal und stilistisch weit weniger vielfältig ausfiel.

Dekoration und Detail wurden mit Ziegelsteinen, Mörtel und ornamentalen Lochziegeln aus gebranntem Ton oder Zement umgesetzt. Der Einfluss der Politik ist deutlich ablesbar: Symmetrische Anordnungen, weite Dachüberstände und Veranden im Stil traditioneller vietnamesischer Häuser waren die bevorzugten Gestaltungsmittel. [**7** Versammlungshalle der Hồ Chí Minh-Nationalakademie für Politik und öffentliche Verwaltung (1958) von Nguyễn Ngọc Chân | **8** Museum für Völkerkunde Vietnams (1962) von Hoàng Như Tiếp]

Ab 1970 folgte eine neue Generation von Architekten, die sowohl in Vietnam als auch in Osteuropa ausgebildet worden war. Zusammen mit einigen Architekten aus den sozialistischen Staaten bildeten diese die treibende Kraft hinter dem sogenannten sowjetischen Stil. [**9** Mausoleum für

4

5

6

joined the resistance; however, some also remained in the hope of business opportunities. During this period, only very few buildings of significant artistic value were created, because construction activity was much reduced owing to the war. Art Deco remained the predominant style in the cities. Those architects who had followed Hồ Chí Minh worked in the forests, with severely restricted resources. There they created a new style: in view of the fact that neither machines nor skilled workers were available, they constructed buildings with the materials on hand, such as bamboo, clay, and fan palm fronds, using local labor and manual working methods. Many large buildings were constructed in support of the resistance fighters, such as the assembly hall for the Second Congress of the Communist Party, designed by Hoàng Như Tiếp in 1950. This building consisted entirely of bamboo and was over 10 meters high. It provided enough space for several hundred delegates. Its simple design, with an elegant load-bearing structure and bamboo facade, makes it seem like a forerunner of the green architecture of the early twenty-first century.

DIVIDED ARCHITECTURE, 1954–1975

After nine years of fighting against the French occupation forces, which finally ended with the latter's departure after the battle of Điện Biên Phủ, peace had still not been established. The country was split into two parts with opposing ideologies. The battle for the people's right to self-determination, for unification of the country, for the end of foreign interference, dominated the political thinking of many Vietnamese and also that of the architects in both systems. For this reason, Vietnamese architecture of that time was determined by the search for modern solutions with a national character.

In South Vietnam, the market economy, the quickly progressing urbanization, and the inevitable contact with Western culture and technology set the course toward a more diverse development of architectural styles and forms than was possible in the North. Imported materials such as cement, glass, and steel were widely available in construction and offered a wealth of design possibilities.

Likewise, architectural education was influenced by domestic and foreign stimuli. In the South, the Colonial style was largely replaced by the International style. Here too, there was a significant attempt to include elements in the design tailored to the local tropical climate, such as in the Palace of Independence in Saigon (1962) [4] by Ngô Viết Thụ. The simple overall design of the building with

its orthogonal shapes corresponds to the International style. Wide corridors around the workrooms and a large inner courtyard for the President's residential quarters ensure shading and cooling. The brise-soleil system, which is reminiscent of bamboo and window grilles from the Vietnamese building tradition, and the type of ornaments used refer back to the aesthetics typical of the country. Likewise, the National Library of Saigon (1968) [5] by Nguyễn Hữu Thiện manifests national character in the design of the solar screening, which resembles the style of traditional buildings. In this way the library does not appear out of place at all, even though it is built entirely of concrete and is remarkable for its strict orthogonal geometry.

Buildings such as the Vĩnh Nghiêm Pagoda (1971) [6], a reinforced concrete construction, and the assembly hall of Cần Thơ University, also express national character in their pattern language. In North Vietnam, urban development only progressed very slowly during the war. The economy and politics were centralized; the only available commissions were those from the government—there were no private clients, and there was little exchange with Western culture, which is why, prior to 1975, architecture in the North remained much less diversified in terms of conceptual design and style.

The decoration and detailing of buildings were achieved with bricks, mortar, and ornamental hollow bricks made of fired clay or cement. The influence of politics is clearly visible—symmetrical arrangements, wide roof overhangs, and verandahs in the style of traditional Vietnamese houses were the preferred design elements. [**7** Assembly Hall of the Hồ Chí Minh National Academy of Politics and Public Administration (1958) by Nguyễn Ngọc Chân | **8** Museum of Ethnology of Vietnam (1962) by Hoàng Như Tiếp]

From 1970 there was a new generation of architects who had been trained in Vietnam as well as Eastern Europe. Together with some architects from the Socialist countries, they formed the driving force behind the so-called Soviet style. [**9** Mausoleum for Hồ Chí Minh (1975) by Garold Grigorievich Isakovich and B. S. Mezentsev | **10** Culture Palace for the Youth in Hanoi (1976) by Lê Văn Lan]

THE POST-WAR PERIOD, 1975–1986

Even the unification of North and South Vietnam did not really bring about peace. The elimination of the war's consequences, two new conflicts at the country's borders, and a weakened economy and civil society

7

8

9

Hồ Chí Minh (1975) von Garold Grigorievich Isakovich und B. S. Mezentsev | **10** Kulturpalast der Jugend in Hanoi (1976) von Lê Văn Lan]

DIE ZEIT NACH DEM KRIEG, 1975–1986

Auch die Vereinigung von Nord- und Südvietnam brachte noch keinen wirklichen Frieden. Die Beseitigung der Folgen des Krieges, zwei neue Konflikte an den Landesgrenzen sowie eine geschwächte Wirtschaft und Zivilgesellschaft stellten ein substanzielles Hindernis für den Aufbau der Städte dar. Auch der Berufszweig der Architekten befand sich in einer schwierigen Situation: Das Modell der Planwirtschaft bestand fort, Architekten aus dem Südteil des Landes mussten sich an die Kontrolle durch die vereinigte Regierung und das Fehlen eines privaten Wohnungsmarktes gewöhnen. Der sowjetische Stil setzte sich durch und verdrängte das Bedürfnis, der Architektur einen nationalen Charakter zu geben.

Der Hauptfokus lag nun auf staatlichen Wohnungsbauprogrammen, allerdings erfüllte die architektonische Qualität dabei nicht die gewünschten Standards. Architekten und Bauunternehmen versuchten sich an verschiedenen Baumethoden und nutzten handwerkliche Techniken ebenso wie das Bauen mit vorgefertigten Elementen. Eine vier- bis fünfstöckige Bebauung wurde für die Infrastruktur der noch im Aufbau befindlichen Städte als geeignet erachtet. Geringe Investitionen bei einem gleichzeitig hohen Bedarf an Wohneinheiten führten zu einem eher tristen Erscheinungsbild. Auch die bauliche Qualität litt unter dieser Ausgangslage, hinzu kamen fehlende Erfahrung in Gestaltungsfragen, eine uniforme Vorfabrikation der Bauteile sowie ein Mangel an qualifizierten Arbeitern. Die von vornherein gering bemessene Wohnfläche und die Verteilung nach Gehaltsstufen hatten zur Folge, dass für viele, insbesondere für große Familien, nicht ausreichend Platz zur Verfügung stand. Die Konsequenzen sind bis heute spürbar: Illegale Landaneignung und Baumaßnahmen jenseits staatlicher Kontrolle sind weit verbreitet. Die neuen Siedlungsgebiete trugen offiziell den Namen „Gemeinschaftssiedlung", wurden nach sozialistischem Vorbild geplant und boten einige Vorteile, konnten allerdings nur in der Planwirtschaft bestehen. Heute sind beinahe alle unter dem marktwirtschaftlichen Urbanisierungsdruck umgebaut worden.

Im Zuge der Vereinigung wurden die architektonischen Eigenheiten beider Landesteile sehr ausgewogen zusammengeführt. Der International Style im Süden und der sowjetische Stil im Norden hatten viele Gemeinsamkeiten, und die vor 1975 erarbeitete Anpassung beider Stile

an das tropische Klima bot eine erfolgreiche Grundlage für die wechselseitige Beeinflussung. [**11** Friedenstheater (1978) von Huỳnh Tấn Phát]

Die Fortschritte bei der Beseitigung der Kriegsfolgen in Vietnam verkörpert die Sanierung des Bahnhofs von Hanoi (1976) [**12**] von Hoàng Nghĩa Sang in ganz besonderer Weise. Der Eingangsbereich und das Dachgeschoss des alten Bahnhofs, der sich in Ost-West-Richtung erstreckt, waren durch amerikanische Bomben zerstört und dann im sowjetischen Stil wiedererrichtet worden. Um der tropischen Hitze im Sommer entgegenzuwirken, versah der Architekt die Fassade mit einem ornamentalen Sonnenschutz, ein weit auskragender Dachüberstand bietet Schutz vor den in der Region üblichen heftigen Regenfällen. Der Kontrast zwischen dem Eingangsbereich in grauem Beton und der Kolonialarchitektur des in einem gelben Pastellton gehaltenen Bestandsgebäudes war nicht unumstritten, dennoch illustriert dieser Hybrid wie kein anderes Gebäude die Geschichte des modernen Vietnam von Kolonialismus über Krieg und Sozialismus bis hin zur Wiedervereinigung.

DIE POLITIK DER ERNEUERUNG (ĐỔI MỚI)

Die Auswirkungen der wirtschaftlichen Erneuerung und der ideologischen Öffnung spiegeln sich in der zunehmenden architektonischen Vielfalt während der 1990er- und 2000er-Jahre wider. Zahlreiche internationale Anleihen erschienen plötzlich neben der sowjetischen Architektur: vom französischen Kolonialstil des 19. Jahrhunderts über den International Style und die Architektursprache der 1960er-Jahre bis hin zur Post- und Neomoderne der 1980er- und 1990er-Jahre war alles vertreten. Es wirkt so, als wäre die Architekturgeschichte der vorangegangenen hundert Jahre plötzlich und innerhalb von nur zwanzig Jahren in Vietnam wiederaufgeführt worden; das Wirtschaftswachstum und die rapide Verstädterung verwandelten das ganze Land regelrecht in einen überdimensionalen Bauplatz. Die neuen ökonomischen Möglichkeiten bei gleichzeitigem Fehlen städtebaulicher Regularien begünstigten einen architektonischen Individualismus, der im Gegensatz zu den Jahrzehnten baulicher Zurückhaltung steht und zu einem sehr heterogenen Baubestand in den Städten führte.

Innerhalb der ersten zehn Jahre der politischen Erneuerung nahmen öffentliche Investitionen eine wichtige Rolle im Bausektor ein. Staatliche Entwurfsbüros unter der Leitung von Architekten, die sich vor 1985 einen Namen gemacht hatten, behielten eine Monopolstellung bei

10   11

12

represented substantial obstacles to the urban reconstruction. Likewise, the architectural profession was in a difficult situation: the planned economy model persisted, and architects from the south of the country had to get used to being controlled by the unified government and to the absence of a private housing market. The Soviet style prevailed and suppressed any desire to give architecture a national character.

Now the main focus was on state-funded housing programs, although the architectural quality did not meet the specified standards. Both architects and building contractors tried out different construction methods and used manual techniques as well as systems of building with prefabricated elements. For the infrastructure of the towns still undergoing reconstruction, four- to five-story-high buildings were considered suitable. Low investment coupled with high demand for housing units resulted in a rather drab appearance. This scenario also led to poor quality construction; in addition there was a lack of design experience, the prefabrication of building components was very uniform, and qualified workers were lacking. The allocated living area was already small; this and the allocation in accordance with salary level meant that for many, in particular for large families, the housing units were just too small. The consequences can be seen to this day: illegal occupation of land and construction beyond state control are widespread. The new settlements were officially called "community estates"; they were designed in accordance with Socialist examples and had some advantages but could really only exist properly in a planned economy. Today, almost all of them have been converted in response to the pressures of the market economy and the resulting urbanization.

In the course of unification, the special architectural characteristics of both parts of the country were combined in a very measured way. The International style in the South and the Soviet style in the North had many shared elements, and the pre-1975 adaptation of both styles to the tropical climate offered a successful basis for mutual influence. [**11** Theater of Peace (1978) by Huỳnh Tấn Phát]

The restoration of Hanoi Railway Station (1976) [**12**] by Hoàng Nghĩa Sang is a particularly good example of the advances made during the postwar restoration period. The entrance area and the attic story of the old station, which is laid out in an east–west direction, had been destroyed by American bombs and then reconstructed in the Soviet style. In order to counteract the tropical heat in summer, the architect applied ornamental sun screening to the facade; a far-projecting roof overhang provides protection from the heavy rainfall common in the region. The contrast between the entrance area with its gray concrete and the colonial architecture of the existing building with its pastel yellow shade was not without controversy; nevertheless, this hybrid illustrates the history of modern Vietnam, from colonialism through the war and the Socialist era to unification, like no other building.

THE POLITICS OF RENEWAL (ĐỔI MỚI)

The effects of economic renewal and ideological opening-up are reflected in increasing architectural diversity during the 1990s and 2000s. Suddenly, international flavors could be noted alongside Soviet architecture: from the French Colonial style of the nineteenth century to the International style, and from the architectural language of the 1960s through to the postmodernism and neomodernism of the 1980s and 1990s—everything was present. It was as if, suddenly, the architectural history of the previous one hundred years had been revived in Vietnam within the short period of only twenty years; economic growth and rapid urbanization turned virtually the whole country into an oversized construction site. New economic possibilities combined with the absence of urban planning regulations favored an architectural individualism that, in contrast to decades of restraint in construction, led to a very heterogeneous assemblage of buildings in the towns and cities.

During the first ten years of political renewal, public investment played an important role in the construction sector. State-owned design practices, headed by architects who had made a name for themselves prior to 1985, retained a monopoly position with regard to state-funded construction projects. To the end of the 1990s, this situation entrenched the local version of the Soviet style as the predominant architectural school, in particular with regard to projects for government institutions and universities. In response to this way of thinking based on the planned economy of the past, with its extremely formal order, many architects discovered and tested a wide variety of international architectural styles. For the first time, private individuals invested in buildings and were prepared to accept even functionally irrational elements for the sake of creating new visual impressions. [**13** Television tower of Hanoi Radio Television (1992) | **14** The Crazy House in Đà Lạt (1990) by Đặng Việt Nga]

13   14

staatlich finanzierten Bauprojekten. Dieser Umstand etablierte den sowjetischen Stil in seiner lokalen Ausprägung bis Ende der 1990er-Jahre als vorherrschende architektonische Schule, insbesondere bei Projekten für staatliche Ämter und Universitäten. Als Reaktion auf diese Denkweise aus vergangenen, planwirtschaftlichen Zeiten mit ihrer extrem formalen Ordnung entdeckten und testeten viele Architekten die verschiedensten internationalen Architekturstile. Erstmals investierten auch Privatpersonen und waren bereit, sogar funktional Unvernünftiges zu akzeptieren, um neuartige visuelle Eindrücke zu schaffen. [‹ **13** Fernsehturm der Hanoi Radio Television (1992) | ‹ **14** „Das verrückte Haus" in Đà Lạt (1990) von Đặng Việt Nga]

Aus diesen konträren Ansätzen entwickelten sich zwei Lager. Die erste Gruppe begrüßte die formalen Freiheiten, während die zweite Gruppe zu den Ausdrucksformen der Kolonialarchitektur zurückkehrte. Nachdem sich die ideologischen Einschränkungen gelockert hatten, überrascht es wenig, dass auch Regierungsvertreter öffentlich ihre Vorliebe für die imposante Erscheinung und die machtvolle Ausstrahlung der französischen Kolonialgebäude erklärten. Einige kaufmännisch versierte und gestalterisch nachlässige Architekten begriffen die Psychologie des Marktes schnell: Es entstand eine Vielzahl von Wohn- und Bürogebäuden, deren Formen auf skurrile Weise der westlichen Architektur des 18. und 19. Jahrhunderts entlehnt waren.

Das Bedürfnis, einen Nationalcharakter in der Architektur auszudrücken, war zwar nicht verschwunden, stand aber nicht mehr so sehr im Fokus wie in der Zeit des Krieges oder der kolonialen Unterdrückung. An seine Stelle war besonders unter jungen Architekten ein Experimentieren mit westlichen und für sie noch neuen Formen getreten. Bei Projekten auf nationaler Ebene blieb der vielbeschworene Nationalcharakter hingegen weiterhin obligat. Gegen Ende der 1980er- und Anfang der 1990er-Jahre bestand eine Vorliebe für Stützstrukturen nach dem Vorbild traditioneller Holzkonstruktionen. Einige Architekten erforschten Konstruktionsprinzipien, Proportionen und Verbindungsdetails der traditionellen Holzbauweise, um sie in modernen Gebäuden umzusetzen.

Seit dem Ende der 1990er-Jahre bis heute hat sich die Verwendung traditioneller Symbole und Motive weiter verbreitet: Klischeehaft kommen runde Formen, die für den Himmel stehen, und eckige, die die Erde symbolisieren, sowie Dong-Son-Trommeln, gebogene Dächer,

Reisstrohhüte oder Lotus in stilisierter Form zum Einsatz. Nicht nur einheimische Architekten bedienen sich formaler Anleihen traditioneller Bauformen, sondern auch ausländische Architekten, die in Vietnam praktizieren, wie im Falle der Nationalversammlung von gmp. Mit ihrer Grundform aus Kreis und Quadrat, die für Himmel und Erde stehen, folgt die Architektur, so das Büro, einer „in der Geschichte Vietnams stark verankerten Tradition für Symbole und Zeichen".

AUSBLICK

In den ersten Jahren des 21. Jahrhunderts kamen viele ausländische Architekten nach Vietnam und gewannen fast alle wichtigen Ausschreibungen, was nach der Kolonialzeit, dem Krieg und der Teilung sowie den sowjetischen Einflüssen wie eine vierte Welle der Einflussnahme von außen auf die vietnamesische Architektur wirkt. Seit der Fertigstellung von Terminal 1 des Flughafens Nội Bài in Hanoi gab es kein Bauwerk auf nationaler Ebene mehr, bei dem die Planungsleitung einem vietnamesischen Architekten oblag – zeitgenössische Projekte von emblematischem, repräsentativem Charakter wie das National Convention Center[**15**], die Nationalversammlung, das Stadtmuseum von Hanoi[**16**], der Bitexco Financial Tower in HCMC [**17**] oder das Verwaltungszentrum von Đà Nẵng[**18**] stammen durchweg von ausländischen Architekten. Der Grund für diese Entwicklung ist einerseits ein globales Phänomen: Weltweit werden für Gebäude dieser Größenordnung zumeist Entwürfe renommierter internationaler Architekturbüros gefordert. Vietnamesische Auftraggeber bilden hierbei keine Ausnahme. Andererseits verfügen vietnamesische Architekten nach den Jahren der Abschottung und des Embargos über wenig Wissen zum technischen Fortschritt in der Bau- und Gebäudetechnik und haben vergleichsweise wenig Erfahrung mit der Gestaltung komplexer, großmaßstäblicher Bauwerke. Ironischerweise scheint nach der Überwindung des Kolonialismus heute die Globalisierung eine andere Form der kulturellen Hegemonie zu bewirken. Positiv betrachtet entsteht daraus jedoch auch eine Antriebskraft für viele heimische Architekten, sich stärker mit dem kulturellen und klimatischen Kontext auseinanderzusetzen, um ihren Platz in der Globalisierung zu finden.

Dieser Essay ist die gekürzte Version eines Artikels aus: *Arch+* Nr. 226, 11. 2016, S. 24–29.

15

These contrasting approaches developed into two camps. The first group welcomed the freedom of form, whereas the second group returned to the stylistic elements of colonial architecture. Once the ideological restraints had been loosened, it is not surprising that even members of the government publicly declared their preference for the imposing appearance and the powerful presence of the French colonial buildings. Some commercially astute architects who paid only superficial attention to the conceptual aspect of design were quick to understand the market psychology: a great variety of residential and office buildings was created, the visual appearance of which was borrowed from the Western architecture of the eighteenth and nineteenth centuries in bizarre ways.

Although the desire to express a national character in architecture had not disappeared, it was no longer as much in focus as during the times of war and colonial repression. In its place, young architects in particular opted for experimentation with Western forms that were still new to them. For projects at the national level however, the much-vaunted national character was still obligatory. Toward the end of the 1980s and beginning of the 1990s, there was a preference for supporting systems modeled on traditional wooden structures. Some architects researched construction principles, proportions, and connection details of traditional wood construction in order to apply these in modern buildings.

From the end of the 1990s until today, the use of traditional symbols and motifs has continued to spread: round shapes that represent heaven, orthogonal shapes that symbolize earth, Dong Son drums, curved roofs, rice-straw hats, and lotus flowers are used in clichéd and stylized form. Traditional building forms are used not only by domestic architects, but also by foreign architects practicing in Vietnam, as in the case of the National Assembly by gmp. With its basic shape consisting of a circle and a square representing heaven and earth, the architecture—according to the practice—replicates "the tradition of symbols and signs that is strongly anchored in Vietnam's history."

OUTLOOK

In the first years of the twenty-first century, many foreign architects came to Vietnam and won almost all the important commissions—which, after the colonial period, the war and the division of the country, and the Soviet influences, seemed like a fourth wave of foreign influence on Vietnamese architecture. Since the completion of Terminal 1 of Nội Bài International Airport in Hanoi, there has not been a single building at national level where the design management was carried out by a Vietnamese architect; contemporary projects with an emblematic, prestigious character, such as the National Convention Center [15], the National Assembly, the Hanoi Museum [16], the Bitexco Financial Tower in HCMC [17], and the Đà Nẵng Administration Center [18], were all designed by foreign architects. On the one hand, the reason for this development is a global phenomenon: for buildings of this magnitude it is common practice, worldwide, to insist on designs by reputed international architectural practices. Vietnamese clients are no exception in this respect. On the other hand, after years of isolation and embargos, Vietnamese architects have little knowledge of technical progress in the construction and building technology sectors, and have comparatively little experience of the design of large, complex buildings. Ironically, having overcome colonialism, globalization today appears to exert another form of cultural hegemony. Looking at this in a positive way, however, this also encourages and drives local architects to engage more fully with the cultural and climatic context in order to find their place in a globalized world.

This essay is the abridged version of an article published in *Arch+* No. 226, 11.2016, pp. 24–29.

16

17   18

Dokumentation
Documentation

Ansicht von Südwesten mit dem zentralen Eingang am Ba Đình-Platz
und dem VIP-Eingang an der Bắc Sơn-Straße
View from southwest with the central entrance on Ba Đình Square
and the VIP entrance on Bắc Sơn Street

↑   Haupteingang am Ba Đình-Platz   ↗   Detailansicht Haupteingang
     Main entrance on Ba Đình Square   Detail view of main entrance

Blick aus dem Eingangsbereich in das Foyer unter dem Plenarsaal
View from the entrance area into the lobby below the plenary hall

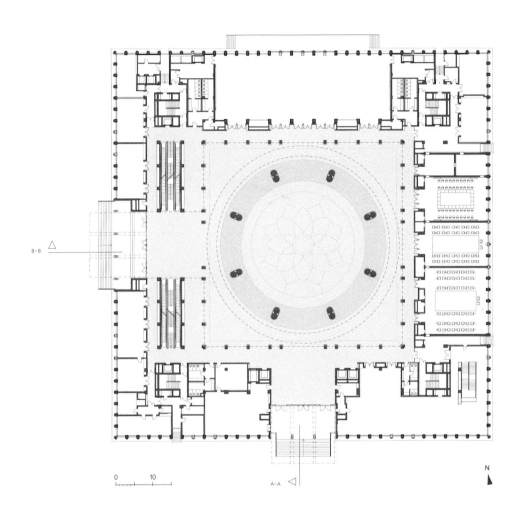

B–B

0   10

A–A

N

Grundriss Ebene 1
Floor plan level 1

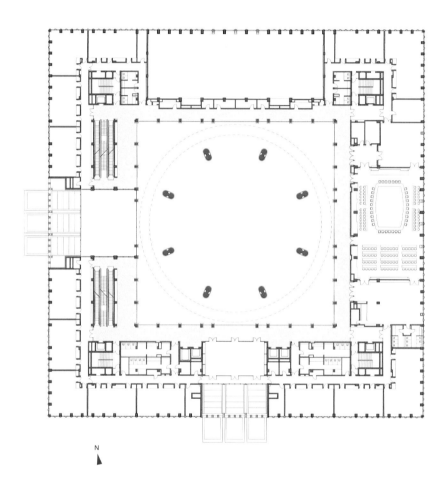

Grundriss Ebene 2
Floor plan level 2

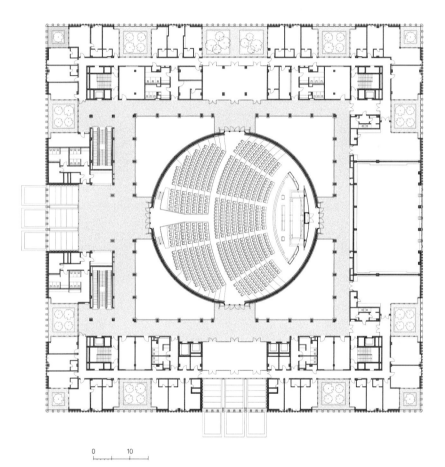

0   10

Grundriss Ebene 3
Floor plan level 3

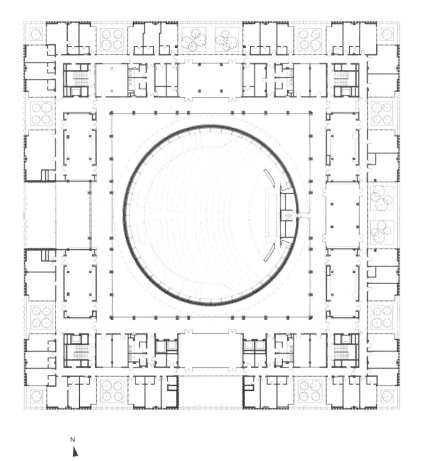

N

Grundriss Ebene 4
Floor plan level 4

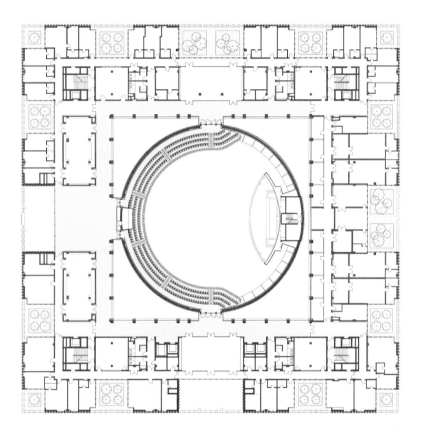

0   10

Grundriss Ebene 5
Floor plan level 5

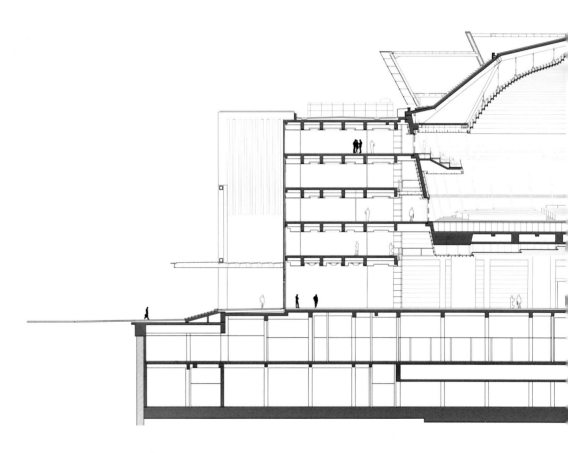

0   10

Schnitt A-A
Section A-A

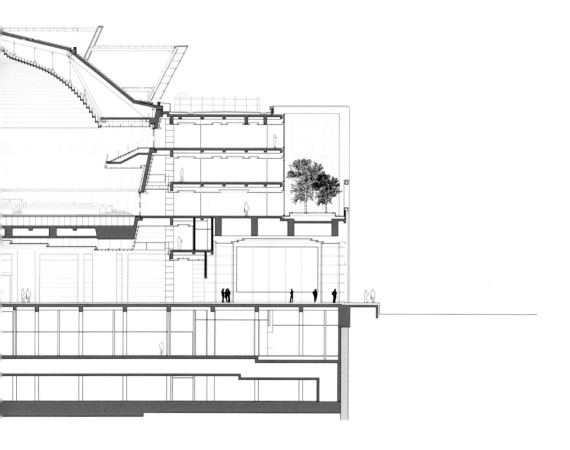

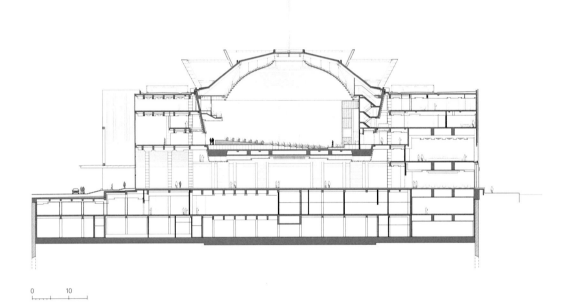

0   10

Schnitt B-B
Section B-B

□ ←   Plenarsaal
       Plenary hall

↑   Galerieebene mit
     340 Sitzplätzen
     Gallery level with
     seating for 340 visitors

↗   Kuppeldecke aus 4500 LEDs und 9400 satinierten
     Glasscheiben, angeordnet in 34 Ringen
     Domed ceiling composed of 4,500 LEDs and
     9,400 satin-finish glass panels arrayed in 34 rings

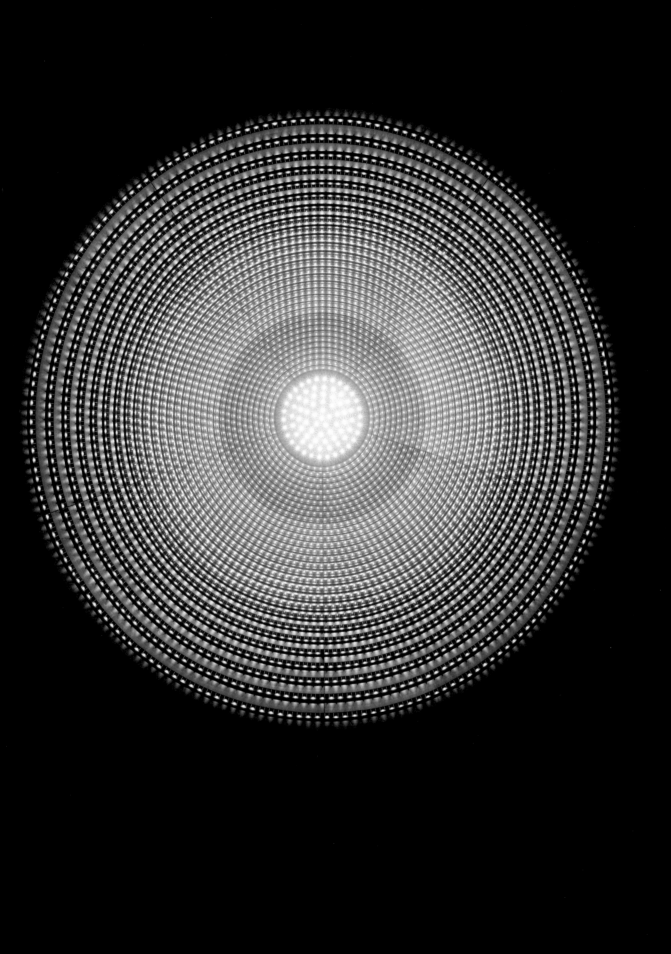

Hinterleuchtete Jadeglas-Fassade des Plenarsaals
Backlit jade-colored glass facade of the plenary hall

Anhang
Appendix

gmp-Entwurfsteam
Design Team

Meinhard von Gerkan
Prof. Dr. h. c. mult. Dipl.-Ing. Architekt BDA

geboren 1935 in Riga, Lettland. Gemeinsam mit
Volkwin Marg gründete Meinhard von Gerkan 1965
gmp · Architekten von Gerkan, Marg und Partner.
Von 1974 bis 2002 hatte von Gerkan den Lehrstuhl
für Entwerfen an der Technischen Universität Braunschweig inne, 2002 verlieh ihm die Philipps-Uni-
versität Marburg, 2005 die Chung Yuan Christian
University die Ehrendoktorwürde. 2007 ernannte
die School of Design der East China Normal University in Shanghai von Gerkan zum Ehrenprofessor,
seit 2014 ist er Advising Professor der Tongji University in Shanghai. Von Gerkan ist Mitbegründer
der gmp-Stiftung und der Academy for Architectural Culture (aac) und hat zahlreiche Auszeichnungen
erhalten, darunter den Rumänischen Staatspreis,
den Großen Preis des Bundes Deutscher Architekten, das Bundesverdienstkreuz 1. Klasse und den
Liang-Sicheng-Preis der Architectural Society
of China. Zu seinen bekanntesten Projekten zählen
der Flughafen Berlin-Tegel, der Berliner Haupt-
bahnhof, die Villa Guna im lettischen Jūrmala,
das Hanoi Museum, das Grand Theater in Chongqing, der Neu- und Umbau des Chinesischen
Nationalmuseums in Peking und die Planung der
Stadt Lingang New City (heute Nanhui New City)
bei Shanghai.

Born in 1935 in Riga, Latvia. In 1965, together with
Volkwin Marg, Meinhard von Gerkan founded gmp ·
von Gerkan, Marg and Partners Architects. From
1974 to 2002, von Gerkan held the Chair of Architectural Design at the Technical University of Braunschweig. He was awarded an honorary doctorate by
Philipps University in Marburg in 2002 and also by
Chung Yuan Christian University in 2005. In 2007,
the School of Design of East China Normal University in Shanghai awarded von Gerkan an honorary
professorship and, since 2014, he has been Advising Professor at Tongji University in Shanghai. Von
Gerkan is a co-founder of the gmp Foundation and
the Academy for Architectural Culture (aac), and
he has received numerous awards, including the
Romanian State prize, the Grand Award of the German Association of Architects, the Federal Cross of
Merit, 1st class, and the Liang Sicheng Prize of the
Architectural Society of China. His best known
projects include Berlin-Tegel Airport, Berlin Main
Railway Station, Villa Guna in Jūrmala, Latvia, the
Hanoi Museum, the Grand Theater in Chongqing,
the reconstruction and renovation of the National
Museum of China in Beijing, and the master plan
of Lingang New City (today Nanhui New City) near
Shanghai.

Nikolaus Goetze
Dipl.-Ing. Architekt BDA

geboren 1958 in Krefeld. Nach seinem Architektur-
diplom an der RWTH Aachen kam Nikolaus Goetze
1987 zu gmp · Architekten von Gerkan, Marg und
Partner; seit 1998 ist er Partner. 2019 lehrte Goetze
als Gastprofessor an der Tongji University in Shanghai. Als Mitinitiator leitet er regelmäßig Workshops
der Academy for Architectural Culture (aac). Zu
Goetzes bekanntesten internationalen Projekten
gehören das Guangxi Culture & Art Center, das
Grand Theater in Chongqing, die Masterplanung
der Stadt Lingang New City (heute Nanhui New City)
und das dortige China Maritime Museum, das Hanoi
Museum sowie das Deutsche Haus in Ho-Chi-Minh-
Stadt. Renommierte Projekte in Deutschland sind
der Erweiterungsneubau für die Kunsthalle Mannheim, das Designzentrum für Audi in Ingolstadt und
das Springer Quartier in Hamburg.

Born in 1958 in Krefeld, Germany. Having completed his architectural studies at Aachen Technical University, Nikolaus Goetze joined gmp · von Gerkan,
Marg and Partners Architects in 1987, where he has
been a partner since 1998. In 2019, Goetze was ap-
pointed Visiting Professor at Tongji University in
Shanghai. As a co-initiator of the Academy for Architectural Culture (aac), he regularly leads workshops
there. Goetze's best known international projects
include the Guangxi Culture & Art Center, the Grand
Theater in Chongqing, the master plan for Lingang
New City (today Nanhui New City), and the China
Maritime Museum there, the Hanoi Museum, and
Deutsches Haus in Ho Chi Minh City, Vietnam. Important projects in Germany include the extension
to Kunsthalle Mannheim, the Audi Design Center in
Ingolstadt, and the Springer Quartier in Hamburg.

Dirk Heller
Dipl.-Ing. (FH) Architekt

geboren 1954 in Soest. Nach einem Studium an
der Staatlichen Akademie der Bildenden Künste in
Stuttgart schloss Dirk Heller 1987 sein Architektur-
studium an der Fachhochschule Hamburg ab und
kam zu gmp · Architekten von Gerkan, Marg und
Partner, wo er seit 2009 assoziierter Partner ist.
Unter seiner Projektleitung wurden neben der Vietnamesischen Nationalversammlung in Hanoi unter
anderem das Culture & Art Center in Guangxi, China, das Landeskirchliche Archiv der evangelisch-
lutherischen Kirche in Bayern in Nürnberg, die Twin
Towers in Dalian, China, das Museum und Archiv
für Stadtentwicklung in Shanghai-Pudong und das
Internationale Messe- und Kongresszentrum in Nanning realisiert. Aktuell arbeitet er unter anderem
an einem Museum für Kulturgeschichte in Suzhou,
einem neuen Operngebäude in Shanghai-Qingpu
sowie einem neuen Archivgebäude für die Staatlichen Archive Bayerns in Kitzingen.

Born in 1954 in Soest, Germany. After studying at
the State Academy of Fine Arts in Stuttgart, Dirk
Heller completed his architectural studies in 1987 at
Hamburg University of Applied Sciences and then
joined gmp · von Gerkan, Marg and Partners Archi-
tects, where he became Associate Partner in 2009.
He took charge of the project management of
the Vietnamese National Assembly in Hanoi, the
Culture & Art Center in Guangxi, China, the State
Archive of the Evangelical Lutheran Church of
Bavaria in Nuremberg, the Twin Towers in Dalian,
China, the Museum and Archive for Urban Develop-
ment in Shanghai-Pudong, and the International
Convention and Exhibition Center in Nanning. He is
currently working on a museum for cultural history
in Suzhou, a new opera building in Shanghai-Qing-
pu as well as on a new building for Bavaria's State
Archives in Kitzingen, Germany, amongst other proj-
ects.

Projektleitung
Project Management

Marcus Tanzen
Dipl.-Ing. (FH) Architekt

geboren 1970 in Delmenhorst. Marcus Tanzen studierte Architektur an der Fachhochschule in Oldenburg und kam 2002 zu gmp · Architekten von Gerkan, Marg und Partner, wo er als Associate Director tätig ist. Er hat als Projektleiter neben der Vietnamesischen Nationalversammlung in Hanoi zahlreiche weitere Projekte realisiert, darunter das China Maritime Museum in Lingang New City (heute Nanhui New City) und das Hanoi Museum in Vietnam.

Born in 1970 in Delmenhorst, Germany, Marcus Tanzen studied architecture at the Oldenburg University of Applied Sciences and joined gmp · von Gerkan, Marg and Partners Architects in 2002 where he works as Associate Director. He has completed numerous projects as project manager, including the National Assembly House in Hanoi, the China Maritime Museum in Lingang New City (today Nanhui New City) and the Hanoi Museum in Vietnam.

Jörn Ortmann
Dipl.-Ing. Architekt

geboren 1962 in Cuxhaven. Jörn Ortmann studierte Architektur an der Technischen Universität Braunschweig, 1997 kam er zu den Architekten von Gerkan, Marg und Partner, für die er zunächst in Deutschland, dann in China und anschließend von 2008 bis 2015 als Director am Standort Hanoi Projekte plante und umsetzte. 2015 kehrte er nach Hamburg zurück, wo er heute für gmp als Projektleiter tätig ist. Neben der Vietnamesischen Nationalversammlung in Hanoi hat er in projektleitender Funktion unter anderem den Christus-Pavillon zur Expo 2000 in Hannover und das Siemens Center in Shanghai realisiert. Aktuell arbeitet Ortmann an der Sanierung und Erweiterung der Hamburger Alster-Schwimmhalle.

Born in 1962 in Cuxhaven, Jörn Ortmann studied architecture at the Technical University of Braunschweig. In 1997 he joined von Gerkan, Marg and Partners Architects, for whom he planned and implemented projects, first in Germany, then in China, and subsequently as Director at the Hanoi office from 2008 to 2015. In 2015, Ortmann returned to Hamburg, where he now works as a project manager for gmp. In addition to the building for the Vietnamese National Assembly in Hanoi, he also worked in a project management capacity for the Christ Pavilion at Expo 2000 in Hanover and the Siemens Center in Shanghai. Ortmann is currently working on the renovation and expansion of Hamburg's Alster-Schwimmhalle, an indoor swimming pool with protected landmark status.

Autoren und Fotografen
Authors and Photographers

Trương Ngọc Lân
Architekt und Wissenschaftler Architect and scientist

geboren 1974. Trương Ngọc Lân studierte Architektur an der National University of Civil Engineering (NUCE) in Hanoi. Von 1997 bis 2006 war er als leitender Wissenschaftler am Vietnam Institute of Architecture (VIUP) im Bauministerium in Hanoi tätig. Seit 2006 ist er Dozent für Geschichte und Theorie der Architektur an der NUCE. Zusammen mit Hoàng Thúc Hào und Nguyễn Xuân Ngọc gründete er 2003 das in Hanoi ansässige Architekturbüro 1+1>2, dessen Fokus auf sozialer Architektur liegt.

Born 1974. Trương Ngọc Lân studied architecture at the National University of Civil Engineering (NUCE) in Hanoi. From 1997 to 2006 he worked as Lead Scientist at the Vietnam Institute of Architecture (VIUP) within the Ministry for Construction in Hanoi. Since 2006 he has been Assistant Professor for History and Architectural Theory at NUCE. In 2003, together with Hoàng Thúc Hào and Nguyễn Xuân Ngọc, he formed 1+1>2 in Hanoi, an architectural practice focused on social architecture.

Christian Gahl
Fotograf Photographer

geboren 1966 in München. Christian Gahl studierte von 1993 bis 1996 Architektur. Seit 1996 ist er als selbstständiger Architekturfotograf international tätig, unter anderem für die Architekturbüros Hild + K., Toyo Ito, Murphy/Jahn, Rem Koolhaas, HG Merz. Auch Künstler wie Keith Sonnier, Ulrich Rückriem, Walter de Maria oder Institutionen wie das Guggenheim New York, das MoMA New York und die Neue Nationalgalerie Berlin zählen zu seinen Auftraggebern. Publiziert werden seine Bilder unter anderem in *The Architectural Review*, *A+U*, *domus* und der *Neuen Zürcher Zeitung*.

Born in 1966 in Munich, Germany, Christian Gahl studied architecture from 1993 to 1996. Since 1996, he has worked as a freelance architectural photographer undertaking international commissions from architects Hild + K., Toyo Ito, Murphy/Jahn, Rem Koolhaas, and HG Merz. His clients also include artists such as Keith Sonnier, Ulrich Rückriem, Walter de Maria, and institutions such as the Guggenheim New York, the MoMA New York, and the new National Gallery in Berlin. His photographs appear in such prestigious publications as *The Architectural Review*, *A+U*, *domus*, and *Neue Zürcher Zeitung*.

Projektdaten
Project Data

Bauherr Client
Ministry of Construction of the
Socialist Republic of Vietnam

Internationaler Wettbewerb
International Competition
2007 – 1. Preis 1st prize

Entwurf Design
Meinhard von Gerkan und and Nikolaus Goetze
mit with Dirk Heller

Projektleitung Wettbewerb
Competition Lead
Evelyn Pasdzierny

Projektleitung gmp Hamburg
Project Lead for gmp Hamburg
Marcus Tanzen

Projektleitung gmp Hanoi
Construction Supervision Lead for gmp Hanoi
Jörn Ortmann

Repräsentant gmp Hanoi
gmp Hanoi Representative
Duc Tran Cong

Mitarbeit gmp Hanoi
gmp Hanoi Team
Holger Schmücker, Tuyen Tran Viet, Tien Hong
Duong Nguyen, Bui Thi Lan Anh, Luu Mai Trang

Mitarbeit gmp Hamburg (alphabetisch)
gmp Hamburg Team (in alphabetical order)
Deren Akdeniz, Christoph Berle, Hanna Diers,
Nicole Flores, Martin Friedrich, Alexandra Kühne,
Jessica Last, Cordula Neben, Nguyen Minh Duc,
Meike Schmidt, Holger Schmücker, Alexander
Schnieber, Urs Wedekind

In Arbeitsgemeinschaft mit
Joint Venture with
Inros Lackner SE, Rostock (Tragwerk und technische
Gebäudeausrüstung Structural engineering and
building services)

Repräsentant Representative
Otmar Haas

Bauleitung Tragwerk und technische
Gebäudeausrüstung Structural Engineering
and Building Services
Martin Goericke, Christian Timm,
Steffen Schmeiser

Raumakustik Building Acoustics
ADA Acoustics & Media Consultants, Berlin
Prof. Dr. habil Wolfgang Ahnert

Fassadenberatung Facade Consulting
Werner Sobek, Stuttgart

Bauphysik Building Physics
vRP von Rekowski und Partner, Weinheim

Landschaftsplanung Landscaping
Breimann & Bruun, Hamburg

Partnerbüro Vietnam Partner Firm in Vietnam
VNCC, Vietnam National Construction Consultants
Corporation – JSC, Hanoi | CDC, Vietnam Invest-
ment Consulting and Construction Design, Hanoi

Bauzeit Construction Period
2009–2014

BGF GFA
36 000 m²

Bildnachweis
Picture Credits

Herausgeber Editors
Meinhard von Gerkan ᵍᵐᵖ
Nikolaus Goetze ᵍᵐᵖ

Koordination Editorial Direction
Detlef Jessen-Klingenberg ᵍᵐᵖ
Berit Liedtke ᵍᵐᵖ

Layoutkonzept und Satz Layout and Typesetting
wibberenz'design, Tom Wibberenz und
and Hendrik Sichler, Hamburg

Korrektorat Proofreading
Mariangela Palazzi-Williams (e)
Katharina Freisinger (d)

Lektorat Editing
Detlef Jessen-Klingenberg ᵍᵐᵖ (d)
Berit Liedtke ᵍᵐᵖ (d)
David Koralek | ArchiTrans (e)

Übersetzung Translation
David Koralek | ArchiTrans
Hartwin Busch (Essay von essay by Trương Ngọc Lân)

Bildredaktion Picture Editing
Trixi Hansen ᵍᵐᵖ
Berit Liedtke ᵍᵐᵖ

Reproduktion Reproduction
DZA Druckerei zu Altenburg GmbH

Druck und Bindung Print Production and Binding
DZA Druckerei zu Altenburg GmbH

Papier Paper
Arto Satin von by INAPA Deutschland
150 g/m²

Schrift Font
Linotype Avenir Next Pro
Linotype Avenir Next W1G

Bibliografische Information der Deutschen
Nationalbibliothek
Bibliographic information published by
the Deutsche Nationalbibliothek

Die Deutsche Nationalbibliothek verzeichnet
diese Publikation in der Deutschen Nationalbibliografie; detaillierte bibliografische Daten sind
im Internet über http://dnb.d-nb.de abrufbar.
The Deutsche Nationalbibliothek lists this
publication in the Deutsche Nationalbibliografie;
detailed bibliographic data are available on the
internet at http://dnb.d-nb.de.

jovis Verlag GmbH
Lützowstraße 33
10785 Berlin

www.jovis.de

jovis-Bücher sind weltweit im ausgewählten Buch-
handel erhältlich. Informationen zu unserem
internationalen Vertrieb erhalten Sie von Ihrem
Buchhändler oder unter www.jovis.de.
jovis books are available worldwide in select book-
stores. Please contact your nearest bookseller
or visit www.jovis.de for information concerning
your local distribution.

ISBN 978-3-86859-402-7